Broken In God's Grace

Christina Worth

Broken In God's Grace
Copyright © 2018 by Christina Worth.

All rights reserved. Printed in the United States of America. No part of this book may be used or reproduced in any manner whatsoever without written permission except in the case of brief quotations em- bodied in critical articles or reviews.

ISBN: 978-1-948829-13-7
First Edition: November 2018

Published by
Greater Working Women Publishing Company, LLC
www.gwwpublishing.com

10 9 8 7 6 5 4 3 2 1

CONTENTS

Introduction
Chapter 1: Serving Death By My Own Hands   1
Chapter 2: Fatherless Child   7
Chapter 3: Nomadic Living   13
Chapter 4: If Love You is Wrong, I Should Run
              Like Hell   19
Chapter 5: Angel Babies   27
Chapter 6: Simply Being Present   33
Chapter 7: Perfectly Imperfect   37
About the Author

Introduction

Grace is as a manifestation of favor, mercy, and freely given, unmerited favor and love of God. As a verb, it is defined as to do honor or credit to (someone or something) by one's presence.

How often do we look back over lives and think wow? Thinking back over the many situations, whether per-designed or a result of our own choices. We are still here. Whether we felt it or not, God's grace has been with us the entire time.

This is not a 10-step outline or a designated how to book, but a book of vulnerability, encouragement, and reflection. We all have struggles and burdens to bear, but God is so amazing that no matter where we are in our lives His grace is always present including during our victories. One of my favorite scriptures is Psalm 138:3 that states, *"In the day when I cried out, You answered me, and made me bold with strength in my soul."*

As I have meditated on this scripture, I realized that often times we look for God to respond to us in a tangible manner (e.g. through people, by changing our situation immediately, or just given us what we want, etc.) but in many instances God gives us the strength and knowledge to make it through. I pray that as I share snippets of my journey of truth, that they encourage and are a blessing to you on your journey. Remember God loves you so much and so do I.

CHAPTER ONE

Servivng Death By My Own Hands

Life isn't about finding yourself. Life is about discovering who God created you to be.
~unknown~

I made it! A high school graduate with a 3.8 GPA, voted "Who's Who" among American students, a member and officer of numerous clubs, and a starter for our high school basketball team. The hard work has paid off. I am ready to spread my wings and find my way in this new chapter of my life. Although my heart was set on going to Spellman in Atlanta, I knew my mama was not going to allow me to go that far from home. Mama's desire was for me to attend a college only 45 minutes from home and that was a negative for me. There was nothing wrong with the college; it just was not my choice. I was truly just trying to break free of the reins of my mama and granny so I began my independent journey at a college in northern Arkansas about 3 hours from home.

Broken In God's Grace

October 2001, I purchased my very first car with the money I had earned working during the previous summers. I was living it up in my new car, but it was short lived. I had a wreck the winter of 2001. Thankfully, my car was still drivable but it needed some cosmetic work. I called my mama and told her so that she could complete an insurance claim. About a week later, I looked out the window only to realize my car was missing! I panicked! Immediately I called my mama. She informed me that my car had been totaled and the insurance company had picked it up. No one told me though. Back to walking again. Visits from my family were slim to none existent but I had two siblings back home that my mama had to care for.

As time went on I knew, I needed to get a job but transportation was essential so that I could keep a job. I eventually ran into some girls from back home that were going to school here also. By this time the relationship between my mama and I had become extremely strained and truthfully, I did not understand why beyond the fact I did not go to the school she wanted me to attend. I would have moments where I would cry but no one knew of my mental breaks. I had to figure out how to obtain the essentials for myself. I made mention to my guy friend, Shaun, that I needed to figure out how to earn some money. Little did I know what I was about to get myself into.

Shaun told me I could make $500 in one day; of course, I needed to know more. I was to be a courier. Shaun felt having a woman transport the product would be less suspicious. If you have not figured it out by now, Shaun was a dope boy. My first run was a trip to Dallas, which round trip would be a 12-hour drive. Everything that could go wrong went wrong. Upon our (Shuan, myself and two of his friends) arrival to the Dallas airport, we needed to obtain a rental and there were none available. Therefore, I was left in the airport restaurant with a suitcase filled with weed.

It gets better! After three hours of waiting, they finally return with a rental that I now have to drive back to Arkansas with the weed. Keep in mind I had a 7 A.M. class the next morning and by now it is almost midnight. As we hit the road, I was to drive the rental car alone the entire way back. I was beyond exhausted; I let the windows down and turned the radio all the way up. When the police officer clocked my speed, I was driving 105 mph. Before he even got to the car, I was crying and praying because if he discovered the cargo that I was carrying, my life would be over. I told the officer that a close relative was on their deathbed and I was trying to get home, he believed me but stated that because I was driving so fast he would have to give me a ticket. I made the $500 only to have to use it to pay for the speeding ticket. That was my first and last weed transport ever.

I still needed money to take care of myself though, so I learned how to braid hair. Due to only receiving a designated amount on my school card for food, I had to be mindful and use it sparingly. Often times I did not eat. By my junior year, I had moved off campus twice, only to have to return. I did the best I could with managing my finances. I knew that I had to save money, but every dime I received seemed to slip through my fingers. I often allowed others to take advantage of me by being so generous. I did not truly understand budgeting but I knew I needed to do better. I was subconsciously spiraling out of control and feeling more and more alone as the days passed. I became ill and had to go to the school doctor. They ran test and provided the results. I heard the doctor's words but I did not grasp what he was saying. He informed me that I was going through a depression and that I was taking my own life in the worst way possible. By starvation, my body was attempting to feed on itself from the inside out. So many people surrounded me yet no one knew.

    My grades had dropped tremendously and I was on academic suspension. Feeling that I was unable to go home, my friend, Zena, offered for me to come and crash with her and her parents. Now mind you, I made sure to experience the many joys of college life creating some epic memories; being a member of the student government association, traveling, partying and meeting some amazing people along the way. I have no regrets, but things were definitely about to worse. Her parents agreed to allow me to stay with them while I was working, until I could get my own place. One day over Christmas break, I was in the bathroom and her father approached me with a proposition. I could pose nude for pictures that he could sale or be pimped out to his son.

    Little did I know that he had a drug problem and was attempting to use me as a means to maintain his supply. I closed the door and cried. Was there no one on the earth that loved me? I began trying to find somewhere else to go. I could not stay here. I was not safe or at least I did not feel safe. Everyone I called had his or her reason for not being able to come and pick me up. I finally called a guy I knew by the name Aaron. I had meet him about a year prior. I did not really know him well but I was desperate.

He drove all the way from Louisiana to get me, so that I could just sleep in peace. I stayed with Aaron for two weeks and returned to Arkansas prior to the spring semester starting. There was no way that I could stay with my Zena's parents, so I lied to her and crashed in her dorm room for a couple of weeks. I felt like I was the only person in the world where it seemed as though nothing would go right for me. All I wanted was to feel loved and know that not every decision I made was the wrong one. What I was seeking, I was looking in all the wrong places to find it. I was looking for my true self.

But unto every one of us is givin grace according to the measure of the gift of Christ.

Ephesians 4:7

CHAPTER TWO

A Fatherless Child

A father to the fatherless, a defender of widows, Is God in His holy habitation.
Psalms 68:5

O ur parents are human and had lives prior to having children. They give us their very best whether good or bad and most times, they cannot give us what they have not experience themselves. What you do with the supplies you are given in life is up to you. Know that God does not leave us in a state of lack for our needs. If God removed it then He is going to replace it with something better.

The days begin to fly by and I needed to find a solution to my living situation quickly. Something was definitely different, I was extremely moody and I could not begin to explain why. I figured it was just stress. One day, I was hanging out in the room and head eaten all the kosher pickels. Therefore, once Zena got out of class, I asked her if she would take me to the store to buy some more. She said, "Not right now." In that instance all of my feelings were hurt and I became very upset with her with tears in my eyes. She looked at me and said "Heffa, you better be pregnant because if you're not we're going to fight! You are tripping." My response was, "Pregnant, with what? Emotions, surely not a baby."

Several days later, I received a call from my Aaron in Louisiana and he offered for me to come stay with him until I could get on my feet. Thank God! A week after I was settled in, I thought to myself could Zena be right about my mood swings. I took a test, positive. Whelp, that test was a faulty test because I am not pregnant. At least that is what I believed to be true. There was no way I was pregnant. Two weeks later, I passed out and had to be taken to the hospital where the doctor informed me I was pregnant and extremely dehydrated. My response was "pregnant with what," the doctor just smiled and explained he would be doing an ultrasound.

He zoomed in on the fetus and said there is your baby. I looked at him and said, "Sir, that's not a baby. That's just a popcorn kernel." He came back with my release papers and just smiled. I am sure this was not his first interaction with an extreme case of pregnancy denial. I got home and ten thousand thoughts filled my mind. Aaron and I are not in a relationship. How do I tell my family? What will people think of me? What am I going to do? Especially with my current situation, living with a man I barely know. I do not have the best relationship with my mama, and I have nothing of my own. I finally was able to doze off and the next day I informed Aaron that I was pregnant. He asked me what I wanted to do. I told him, I wanted to keep it.

 Several months had passed and rumors of all sorts were going around back home about my current situation. Yet no one truly had a clue and I still had not told my family about my pregnancy. Finally, Aaron and I went home so that he could meet my family. My grandfather being very traditional, immediately mentioned marriage but that was not our path. Truthfully, I cared for Aaron and had the utmost admiration for him because he was there when I needed him most but I was not in love with him no more than he was in love with me. We both agreed that we would not focus on marriage. Instead, we would see what could happen for the sake of our unborn child. The relationship quickly took a wrong turn. Aaron was becoming more distant and although he would be lying next to me, I would feel completely alone.

 Shortly after our visit home, I received a call from my best friend from back home and she wanted to know if I was handling everything ok. I was confused, so I asked her to clarify. She informed me that my mama had told several people that she would not be dealing with me or my bastard baby. My hormones were already all over the place due to my pregnancy and this was critical blow to my confidence. I already felt alone and those words my mama spoke solidified that loneliness. Mental pep talk "Keep going you got this, don't give up just keep fighting your way through. Jesus loves you."

 June 17, 2004, I was sent home from work due to

having faint and dizzy spells six months into my pregnancy. Once home a relative suggested I should go to the ER. The doctor informed me after arriving that I was in labor. I was having contractions five minutes apart and I felt absolutely nothing. Stopping the labor was essential due to me not even feeling the contractions and my daughter was only eight ounces. To give birth to her in that moment would be terminal for her. I began to pray like never before because to lose her would surely kill me. She was my real-life guardian angel.

The stress from the arguments, moving back and forth, work, and trying to do it all myself had taken its toll. The doctor placed me on a permanent bedrest until after her birth, for her sake and mine. After several hours, my labor ceased and I was released to go home. I went on maternity leave and truly had to reevaluate my current living situation. My grandma called and asked me to come home so that they could take care of me after hearing about my hospital visit. I was still wounded from the words I was told my mama said, but it was not about me but my princess.

Around the first part of August, while my daughter's father was away for the weekend with another woman, whom I knew about. My stepfather and stepbrother came, helped me with my belongings, and took me back home. I told very few people that I was leaving because I did not want Aaron to know where I was. August 17, 2004, my princess arrived four weeks premature, weighing 4lbs 11ounces at 11:57A.M., and she was absolutely perfect. The unconditional love that I longed for, I finally had it with her.

Not having my father in my life consistently played a

part in some of my insecurities but God did not leave me in lack of influential males in my life. For me because it wasn't my dad, I felt as though I didn't have as others did but I was blessed to have my great grandfather, grandfather, stepdad, along with uncles and cousins who looked out for me. I was so busy focusing on what I did not have that I could not grasp the magnitude of what I did have. Thinking about my own dad's absence, I did not want my daughter to experience the same thing, so I endured many toxic interactions with her father. Once I realized that everything she needed God would provide, I was able to let go and let God.

    This thought process did not happen overnight. There were still unsuccessful interactions that occurred over the years with Aaron, but each one made me stronger. It all helped me to accept whether Aaron was present in her life or not. As long as I knew I was giving her my all, God would do the rest. Aaron was not a bad person, just not the right person for me. My daughter became my top priority and showing her that no matter what she could be anything she wanted to be became my goal in life. Every time you think that you are taking a loss, know God is preparing to bless you with something better. Positive perspective is key.

But he giveth more grace. Wherefore he saith, god resist the proud, but giveth grace to the humble.

James 4:6

CHAPTER THREE

Nomadic Living

Nomad: a person who does not stay long in the same place; a wanderer.

After my princess was born, we stayed with my family for a little over a year in Arkansas. Within that years' time, I experienced something I had never heard of before; church hurt. Growing up in the south there are many traditions of the church. One of those was asking the church for forgiveness when publicly stepping outside of God's will. Having my princess out of wedlock (not married), the notion to apologize to the church was swarming around me from all angles. I finally gave in but in my mind, I only needed to ask God for forgiveness, not a group of individuals of whom many were still comfortable functioning in their own sins.

I stood before the church, apologized, and was baptized again at the age of 21. People shouted and praised God, including my mama, all the while, I stood there feeling persecuted and judged. I already knew that I was wrong and accepted full responsibility for my actions. The last thing I needed was to feel as though I was a walking billboard for being disobedient to God. My granny would say it is like the pot calling the kettle black. They had sinned and many were sinning. Yet they were convinced that without me doing this, I was damned to hell. I was amongst a bunch of holier than thou secret sinners and I could not have felt more alone. What I needed and what was given definitely did not align.

Shortly after that, I knew it was time for my princess and me to find our way. Even though I truly did not have everything figured out, I knew being in Arkansas was not it. First, I had to go back to school and obtain my degree. I was the primary example for my baby girl and I had to show her that the only boundaries we have in life are the ones we place on ourselves. I began the process to get back into school, just to learn, that only six of my college credits would transfer to the college in Louisiana. I could either return to my previous college in northern Arkansas as a junior or start over as a freshman in Louisiana.

I cried that day because the best decision for us would require me to start over and I really did not want to do that. Louisiana was the more rational decision for my baby girl, so I started over as a freshman in August 2005. I had to have an extreme pep talk with myself because my confidence was taking another hit. I could not allow myself to fall into a dark place because it was not just me anymore. I got a job at a newly built movie theater and found a roommate by the name of Diamond. Things were really rough, but I was determined to do it on my own, I did not want either of us to be a burden to anyone. My biweekly minimum wage pay was not even close to being enough for me to survive on my own and especially not with a baby. She needed diapers, milk and clothes not to mention the basic essentials I needed for my daily upkeep. I did not have the money so something had to give. I would never let my baby go without her necessities.

  Diamond was somewhat roguish and street smart. She had a boyfriend and two little ones of her own. I spoke of my dilemma to Diamond and her response was that she had a hookup at a nearby store. We picked a date and time to go to the store when her friend would be working the register. The security would be a one-man show or none at all and management would not be present. When the day came, I had already mentally prepared myself to get in and get out. We established a timeframe to be in and out. We entered the store; I grabbed a shopping buggy and proceeded to find the largest storage tub I could. I then found all the essentials needed for my princess and I, placing them inside the tub and covering it with the lid.

  My heart felt as though it would come out of my chest as I waited in the checkout line. Finally, I was at the register, she scanned the bar code on top, never picking up the tub. I paid for the tub and was out the door. I made my way to the far end of the parking lot and waited for Diamond who had gotten cold feet while inside. Now this was her idea and she got cold feet. What the hell?! My thought process was get in, get out and do not get caught. This was my first and last time. I was not about that life at all.

  It caused me to make a decision that shook me more than anything and that was sending my princess back to my mama and granny while I got on my feet. She was my lifeline and every time I felt like I just could not go on, to look at her and see that smile helped me to find strength I did not even know I had. I will never stop telling the world that God gave me her to save me. Her well-being was a top priority and the only way I could make sure of that was to step outside of myself. I wanted to keep her with me but that was not what was best and although my mama and I did not have the best relationship, I knew my princess would be safe with her.

  I begin to move around from place to place, staying with people whom I had crossed paths with and were kind enough to lend me their couch or maybe even a spare bed. I would never stay too long because I did not want to wear out my welcome. This was tiresome. I had crashed at a home girl's house one night only to wake up to a stranger at my feet. My first reaction was to attempt to break his face with my foot. I did not sleep the rest of the night and that was my last night there. I still did not have reliable transportation so I would always try to find somewhere near my job because I generally would walk to work. I eventually moved in with some coworkers and their grandma. They allowed me to stay rent-free as long as I did not mind helping look after their granny.

  I slept in the room with her and for the first time in a while, I felt safe. I loved waking up to her looking at me, and I am sure she was wondering when I would wake up so she could talk to me. Lol Being in her presence was a blessing to me far beyond anything I could imagine at that time. I eventually got another job and was able to purchase a reliable cash car. The time had come for me to move out because I had gotten my own apartment and another job. I now worked at a home improvement store. I was not at this job two weeks before I meet a young woman named Jasmine, who was destined to become one of my best friends.

    Although I had my own apartment, I could not afford to have the lights turned on yet, absolutely no furniture and little to no food but that did not stop me. I was in my own place with peace of mind. One day at the end of our shift, Jasmine asked me what I was eating for dinner. She had no clue of my situation and that many days I was starving because I could not afford anything to eat. I did not desire to be anyone's charity case. I had to learn the difference from needing a hand up and asking for or seeking handouts. I never wanted to be seen as someone looking for a handout but if you are in need and you do not ask. How will anyone know? Every day she would bring me lunch and I would have dinner with her and her family. I slowly began to be able to put groceries and furniture in my apartment little by little. I was starting to gain my balance in this journey called life. I have always been beyond grateful for the earth angels I have met throughout my journey. They were simply God's way of reminding me that during my dark moments His grace was still very present.

And of his fullness have all we received, and grace for grace.

John 1:16

CHAPTER FOUR

If Loving You Is Wrong, I Should Run Like Hell…

At your absolute best, you still won't be enough for the wrong person. At your worst, you'll be worth it to the right person…
~ Unknown~

Things are finally falling into place. My apartment is furnished and I have a reliable vehicle. Although I did not reside in the best part of town, only having to pay $325 for rent was all I could afford yet I viewed it as an absolute blessing to me. My princess was back with me and I was able to obtain food stamps and childcare from the government while I was getting my balance in this thing called life. My routine consisted of school, work and my princess. It was she and I against the world and that was all right with me. I was on a mission to give her the absolute best life had to offer no matter what.

Broken In God's Grace

A girlfriend Leila decided that she wanted to publish a calendar and asked me and another mutual friend of ours if we would participate. After having my baby girl, I was really self-conscious about my body. I did not think I had the body for a calendar but out of love and respect for her, I agreed. We finished the swimwear shoot and I was relieved. This was totally outside of my comfort zone, yet an amazing experience. I received a call from Leila telling me that we would have to redo the shoot because someone leaked some of the photos. Why Lord?! I barely made it through the first shoot, now we have to do another one but there was no way I would just leave her hanging especially since it meant so much to her.

She wanted this shoot to be more risqué so our outfits went from bathing suits to lingerie. I had never worn lingerie before; therefore, it took me more time to figure out how to put it on than it did to put it on. Real life struggles!! Lol I survived the second shoot, printing was complete and it was now time for distribution. What good is distribution without a meet and greet for the public to see the calendar girls face to face. The event took place at one of the hot spots in town. While signing calendars, a gentleman walks up to me and says, "I would like your autograph and your phone number." As I looked up, I realized it was a guy knew by the name of Ray.

Ray and I had meet about a year and a half prior and would just speak in passing nothing more. He was tall, handsome, funny, smart and currently in the military. I gave him my number and we went for breakfast after the event was over to catch up. He took me home only for me to find that my car had been broken into. The culprit took my stereo, spare clothes, shoes and even my underwear. Really, my underwear! Now dammit people should have limits but I guess not. Ray stayed with me that night and we sat on the sofa and talked until I fell asleep. He had just returned from being stationed in Alaska and his new location was at a base in southwest Texas. We began communicating with each other almost every other day. We would take the time to see each other every chance we got when he was in town to see his family.

Now in life there are always signs (red flags) that you see when dealing with people. Some are subtle while others are like an advertisement sign, big and bold. I had always dreamed of obtaining my degree, getting married, buying a home, owning my own business and having children. In that order. Whelp, if you have not figured it out, I was obviously reaching these goals backwards. Nevertheless, things seemed to be turning around for me. Ray and I were officially dating now. After coming home to visit one weekend and returning to base, Ray called stating he was experiencing symptoms that sounded like a urinary tract infection; it could not possibly be anything else. Right?! So of course, I recommended he go to the doctor.

He calls me later that day to inform me of what the doctor's diagnosis was. To my surprise, he states that he had an STD, which the doctor informed him he had had it for a while and I needed to go get check. (red flag) I was angry, scared and ready to fight all at the same time. Ray pleaded with me that he had not been with anyone else since he and I started dating. I believed him and stayed. Thankfully, my results came back negative. Months went by and everything seemed to be going perfect, I even got the job I had been praying for with the prominent cellular company. It was October and I would need to complete training in north Texas before I could start working. The weekend prior, I spent with Ray, as I was preparing to leave him, something seemed to be wrong. I asked if he was okay and he said, "Yes," so I left it alone. We said our see you laters and I called him once I made it to my destination, but he did not answer.

Several days went by and still nothing. I called his sister Rosalyn and she informed me she had spoken with him earlier that day. I did not understand what was happening; we had just seen each other. Several more days went by and I received an email. In this email, Ray proceeds to tell me that he could no longer talk to me because one of his home girls from high school told him that I had been harassing her and he does not deal with drama like that. (Red Flag) I had no knowledge of the female and had never seen or meet the young woman. Although I was completely confused and my feelings were hurt, I proceeded forward and left him alone.

It had been over a month and I was doing fine. I would talk with his sisters quite often; we had established a relationship outside of my relationship with Ray. Christmas was about 10 days away and Ray's sister Rosalyn and I were catching up over the phone. She happened to mention that Ray was feeling down because he would not be able to make it home due to lack of finances and everyone on base would be going home. Now God gives us all common sense but often times when the heart is involved, the heart will dominate. There is a big difference between being forgiving and being foolish. In this instance, Ray had shown me who he was and I foolishly made my decision. God will often remove things and people from our lives because He knows they are no good for us but if we just cannot seem to let go then He will allow us to have it so that we can truly see exactly why we did not need it in the first place.

I was honestly not over Ray so I went to pick him up and his sister and cousin rode with me. We made through the holidays and he and I were an item again. Second time is the charm at least that is what I had heard. Things were going great, Ray has received a promotion and we have talked about marriage as well as him adopting my princess. March 2008, Ray found out he would be deployed to Iraq for 18 months so our plans were to get married after he returned. Ray informed me that he would have to complete a training before his promotion would be valid. He completed the training and returned home two weeks before my 25th birthday.

While he was in town, we got into a disagreement about him not coming home especially since he was in town for a couple of days before he had to report to his new base. He whispered sweet nothings again and then he was off to base. My gut was telling me that something was coming, I really did not know what it was but from the eerie feeling I had I was not eager for its arrival. The week after my 25th birthday, I received a call from a friend while I was at work. She told me that Ray had gotten married. This cannot be. I just saw him a couple of weeks prior. We made future plans and I did my absolute best to be all that he needed and more. He loved me. He would not do something like this to me. I began to call his sister Rosalyn, his sister in law, his mom and him. I was calling everyone and no one was answering.

I finally got Ray on the phone and asked him, he reluctantly answered me, acknowledging that he was married. When I asked why, his response was that he and the young woman had an agreement. What the hell did that mean? An agreement, marriage is so much more than that. What could I have possibly done in life to deserve this? I try to be the best person I can, I have minimized myself in effort to try to be all that others desire of me. Why me?? Everything around me stopped. I had collapsed and my coworkers were attempting to revive me.

As I came to myself, I heard a voice say check your account. Ray and I had a joint account, but he was not very savvy financially. I found our account over five hundred dollars in the negative because he purchased the ring for his new wife out of our account with his card. This was the worst nightmare ever and I just wanted to wake up but I could not. I was now angry and I wanted to see Ray face to face. I only had a half a tank of gas so I asked my friends for gas money, none of them thankfully gave it to me. For in my irrational state I had plan to whip Ray's ass and blow up his truck which I had pretty much paid for, but he wasn't worth it.

For three weeks, I functioned in darkness, except for school and work. Even at those places, I was simply on autopilot. I had cut off all communication and I would come home and just sleep. I wanted to blame Ray for everything but I could not. The signs were there and I chose to ignore them. God tried to warn me without devastation but I had to learn the hard way so that I would not go back. Finally, one day I heard a voice say, "That's enough. It's time for you to come back." I did not truly understand the meaning of guarding my heart, but I was learning. I realized there must be a healthy balance between loving others and loving yourself. I cried my last tear that day for the relationship I had with Ray and regained focus to reach my goals. Being with someone who truly loves you, will never require you to diminish your value or belittle you. Know that you are worth fighting for. Someone is praying for a person just like you, flaws and all, so do not lose hope.

Let us there fore come boldly unto the throne of grace, that we ma obtain mercy, and find grace to help in timeof need.

Hebrews 4:16

CHAPTER FIVE

Angel Babies

I am sitting at the bar of one of my favorite hangout spots in the Red River District with my cousin Monique. There is this cute gentleman sitting at the end of the bar all alone. I asked the bartender, who was a friend of ours, who the guy was. During this time my cousin had made her way to the end of the bar talking to him and gesturing towards me. Now I was simply just admiring the scenery with no other plan in mind. I just thought he was cute. I surely was not in any rush to get into a relationship with anyone. He made his way down to where we were sitting and introduced himself as Ben.

Ben was two years younger than me, with no children, never married, currently attending the same university as I was, and I almost forgot to mention he was in the military also. I had my reservations about men in the military due to my last relationship but I could not hold him accountable for something he knew nothing about. I did not intend to make the same mistake with Ben that I made with

Ray and not pay attention to the signs, so I took my time in getting to know him. We began talking to each other more and more, even falling asleep talking on the phone. We began dating and he knew exactly what he wanted or so I thought. He told me he felt that I was the one and he wanted to meet my family and my princess. I had to decline because I wanted to make sure that this would be something that would last.

Introducing him to my princess prior to knowing for sure was out of the question. Walking out or hurting me was one thing but to do that to her was not an option. He was not happy with my response but he understood. Although he understood, he was still determined to get what he wanted. We were around each other as much as possible. A week before Christmas I found out I was pregnant. I was both happy and sad about it. Happy because I wanted more children and sad because I still was not married. Granted Ben was all for us having a future together and having children, but I did not want it like this.

As I was dialing his number, this eerie feeling came over me that I just could not explain. I ignored it and felt it was the baby. Ben answered his phone and I told him I was pregnant. He responded by saying, "Wow, I'm not ready." I responded, "What the hell do you mean you are not ready? You had to be ready for something because that is how we got here." I felt as though I had consistently walked into brick walls and I mentally, physically and emotionally could not take it anymore. I had sworn that I would never have an abortion but you have to be careful of saying what you will never do. Life has a way of placing you in situations where you will have to face that "never" situation.

I am a single mother in school, who isn't financially stable, lacking a strong support group, lacking a positive relationship with my daughter's father, and Ben whom I thought had it all together is proving me wrong. Do I bring this child into the world in hopes that eight months from now Ben will be ready for the responsibility of a family or what? I was slowly going back into that dark place again because the decision I was about to make would leave me feeling numb. I called Ben and informed him of my decision, he stated the final decision was for me to make anyway, and he would split the cost with me and take me to the clinic. I completed the screening process. As I heard the heartbeat, a piece of me died.

This was my baby boy, although not fully developed I knew this was my baby boy. His name would have been Thomas James (TJ), a strong, intelligent, proud name just as he would have been. My appointment was December 30 and Ben arrived to pick me up. As we arrived to the clinic, I began to get sick to my stomach but while we were waiting, Ben was acting as though nothing out of the ordinary was happening. They called my name and as I walked back, my body seemed to become heavier with every step. They gave me medication to help me relax but I could still hear the machines. When it was all over and I was home, I prayed pleading and asking God and my precious baby boy to forgive me for trying to do what I thought was best for him and his sister.

I did not tell my family about the pregnancy. I did not need any more judgement because I had already placed judgement upon myself and would have to live with it for the rest of my life. As long as I had my princess and Ben, I can get through this. I called Ben the following day only to get his voicemail. Four months had passed and Ben was nowhere. God, I know I am strong and you make no mistakes but why me??? Who will be there for me? Am I asking too much of someone to be consistent and dependable? To be truthful and loving, not because they feel they have to be but because they want to be and I deserve that. I give a 110% only to barely get 25% in return. I have to figure this thing called life out. I was starting to find my way again and one day my phone rings. I answered it was Ben.

  Now this bastard has the audacity to call me after all this time. He begins by telling me he was involved with a legal situation that was still pending but per his lawyer's instructions, he cannot disclose any information about to me. Then why are you talking to me was my next question. My hurt and pain resurfaced again and I cursed him out, explaining to him where he needed to go and how to get there. He allowed me to vent and proceeded to say that he wants us to get married and have a family. I calmed myself and explained to him that he left me when I needed him most. My abandonment issues were at an all-time high with him. He had to prove himself worthy of being a husband, father and even a friend. I will do whatever it takes, he said.

  Things seemed to be progressing for the better, until I called him one day because I had not heard from him all day. Two days had go by and nothing, I was beginning to think he had went MIA again. My phone rings, its Ben, I immediately go into attack mode. He finally gets me to calm down enough for him to tell me that he was involved in a motorcycle accident, which resulted in several bruised bones and extreme road rash. Although I was upset with him, I did not want anything bad to happen to him. I dropped everything and went to his side. I still needed him to understand what was required of both of us, if marriage was ever to be an option.

I helped nurse him back to good health and we seemed to be growing closer together. Only for him to eventually disappear on me again. To my surprise, he was deployed. Shortly after, I found out I was pregnant again. I did not have a clue where Ben was nor any idea of who to contact to reach him. No more, on that day I made up in my mind that I would not let another man get close enough to me to hurt me. I wanted love but it had to be on my standards or I would remove myself from the relationship. I had begun to build a fortress around my heart that would take a touch from God to remove.

I had another abortion and never told Ben or anyone else besides my friend Dawn, who took me to the clinic. My heart was little colder and my view of people was drastically changing. God, you must hate me right now. I still cannot figure life out. I am giving my all yet I continue to ending of with the short end of the stick. My reality check was that even in loving people one has to make wise decisions and pay attention, not everyone deserves to know the full magnitude of your love simply because they will not appreciate it.

But by the grace of God I am what I am...

1 Corithians 15:10a

CHAPTER SIX

Simply Being Present

The past cannot be changed and the future cannot be predicted. Being present allows you to enjoy the simple yet sweetest moments life has to offer even when things are rough. We miss so much because we are distracted by the pain of the past and the fear of the future... Live in your Now and focus on simply being Present...
~ Monica~

Over the next couple of years, life was somewhat of a blur. I did date but as soon as the guy stepped outside of what I thought was ideal, then I would cut him off. School, work and my princess were priority. Nothing else really mattered. In early 2009, my car was broken into while I was at an event for work and my purse, which held my driver's license and social security card, was stolen. Detectives were on the scene because there had been a string of break-ins. Since I was not a permanent resident of Louisiana, I needed to return to Arkansas to replace my stolen documents. I informed the detective of this and he stated that all I needed to do was present his card and explain the situation if needed.

While I was on my way home to replace the documents, an officer stopped me. I politely inquired what was the problem. The officer states that I was speeding. The area I was in at the time was a speed trap because the speed limit signs changed within less than a mile. I did not argue because I just wanted to get home. I explained my situation, providing all my personal information so that he could identify me and showed him the detective's card as instructed. The officer told me that because I did not have proof of my identity, proof of registration, and the fact that I was speeding, all three charges added up to equal a felony. I was going to jail. I had my bestie Jasmine on the phone the entire time because although it was the 21st century, I was still a young black female and he was a white cop.

He proceeded to handcuff me, put me in the back of his car and took me to a maximum-security prison. As I entered the prison, the officer at the desk looked at me and she asked my name. Once I told her, she immediately apologized not because we knew each other yet from my information she knew I was not supposed to be there but because he had entered me into the system, I would have to complete the booking process. They took all my belongings and placed me in general population. An inmate walked up to me and she said, "You don't belong here. You need to call a bail bondsman baby girl." I looked at her puzzled because I thought that the prison set you up with bail bondsman.

The inmate helped me through the process and laughed at me. She told me from the minute I walked through the doors, I stood out like a sore thumb. I appreciated her kindness and her encouraging words. I did not eat nor did I sleep, the idea of staying in jail overnight was not an option. I was booked around 3 P.M. and my cousin, Monique, made my bail and arrived around 2 A.M. Exhausted was an understatement. Later the following day, I had to get my car out of impound which caused me to miss work. Because of all this, I ended up losing my job at the cellular company. I picked up two jobs and worked seven days a week for over a year and a half until graduation.

May 2010, I received my bachelor's degree in Business Administration and Management. The time leading to this day was pretty much a blur; I do not remember assignments, group activities, talks with friends or even simplest moments of my baby girl growing up right before my eyes. One thing was for sure, I was walking across that stage if it was the last thing I did. Now, I had zoned in on graduating so much so that I had not really thought about after graduation goals. Relocation was on the top of the list so that I could be in position for more opportunities.

The next two years consisted of me going on a wild goose chase and I did not have a clue what I was chasing nor who I was. I was moving through life in a fast forward mode attempting to hit all the high points while missing all the small details. I had guardian angels with me the entire way and many of them I saw on a daily basis but I did not know it then. In addition to what had already happened during these years, I lost one of my younger brothers. Everything I owned was repossessed once I relocated and I was letting everyone that I loved down. I was so busy being strong that I truly did not even know how to react too many of the experiences I encountered.

      Although I was stubborn and hardheaded, God was still giving me testimonies while continuously attempting to get my attention. As I think back over those years, those blurred periods remind me to not only appreciate the moment but to appreciate the people also. Now is defined as at the present moment or time. Yesterday is gone and tomorrow has not yet arrived so dance whether it be sunshine, rain, sleet, snow, or even hurricane. Whatever your current situation is thank God for allowing you to be present in your now! I will not say it is easy but it is definitely worth it.

CHAPTER SEVEN

Perfectly Imperfect

Many often think of being broken as a negative thing, because for most it means we are in a vulnerable position and I was one of the many. I felt as though I had to always seem as if I had it all together and exhibit nothing but strength. As I move through this thing called life, I have gained an unimaginable appreciation for my broken places. Have you ever broken a glass and attempted to glue it back together? If you hold it up to the light, it will reflect the most mesmerizing rainbow of colors. Being broken in God's grace is the best place to be. It allows the master carpenter to piece you back together exactly as He designed for you to be.

    I have struggled with low self-esteem and depression for many years in my life, but I had perfected the ability to smile my way through every situation and not show weakness, so I thought! Truth is the harder I try to hide it, the more visible it became. It did not happen overnight but it definitely happened. Once I could not hide it anymore, I began to isolate myself. People around me did not realize that I often did not even trust my own judgement. Although I did my best to make the best decision for everyone involved, it always seemed as though I could not win for losing.

Simply put I was always wrong. Growing up with my granny and mama, they had their idea of exactly how I was to live my life but I was fighting extremely hard to find myself and just be me. I was disowned for having a baby out of wedlock, called an unfit parent, accused of stealing from my mama and even talked about mostly by those I was striving to please. All of this sent me on a relentless journey for perfection. It resulted in me often allowing others to minimize me to their idea of who I was but that was about to change.

In late 2012, I ran into a friend from back home in Arkansas. He and I had not seen each other in years but would randomly reach out to see how the other was doing. We began hanging out with each other, every week, several times a week. I was beginning to think he was the one but being mindful of my past I did not want to rush anything. Things seemed to be going well, until Feb 2013 when a picture of him and another young woman appeared on social media. Of course, I inquired and his response, oh she's just a friend.

He became more distant and even had ignored me in the mall while with some coworkers because, he and the young woman were more than just friends. Everyone knew that except me. I was truly hoping that I could trust him. I still treated him as a friend and yes, by this time we had been intimate prior to my knowledge of the other woman. I stepped back and went on with my life but things had been rough for me. My depression was getting the best of me and I was feeling all alone. One day after work, I could not deal with it any more. This was it. This would be the day I would take my life. The world would not miss me. I did not keep weapons or medicine in the house because of my daughter. We had no cleaning supplies because I needed to go shopping. Last resort was that we lived on the third floor and I could just jump. I sat down to get my thoughts together of how to accomplish my goal. A gentle voice filled the room saying, "You were made on purpose with a purpose, fearfully and wonderfully made in My image. I just need you to love yourself the way I love you." (God) I got up, looked in the mirror and began to reevaluate the woman I saw. My next question to God was of course, "What is my purpose?"

  I began the journey of becoming who God had created me to be. A life without distractions is no life at all, so of course, my friend from Arkansas appeared again with a lame story but I fell for it. (side eye) 2014 was intense and another woman surfaced that was just a friend but this was the last time. As I began to fall in love with myself, my so-called friend and his behavior became an absolute unnecessary pain in the butt. At this point I asked God to give me the strength to move forward and to leave this situation better than when I entered it.

  Early 2015, God told me it was time to relocate. In June, we moved back to Dallas. I had learned my lesson to wait on Him, so my prayer went like this, "Lord I don't want to be outside of your will anymore. I want all that you have destined for me so I will get out of the way and allow you to lead. I do not want to miss my blessings anymore. I am going to sit still and await Your directions. I desire a home, a career job, to be debt free, financial stability and a husband after your own heart that will pursue and love me the way you love the church."

Over the past two years, my nonprofit has flourished, I have a job that I can pursue as a career, and I am working towards owning my own home and being debt free. I am continuously striving to be better every day . Do I have it all together? Nooo, not at all. Am I perfect? Nope and I do not even desire to be but I do desire to be the best that God has designed for me to be. Am I enjoying the adventures along the journey? I can't say that every adventure is enjoyable, but I have learned to appreciate the beauty and lessons that come with each one. Not saying that every day is a sunny day but even on my rainy days, I honestly have a reason to smile.

Loving yourself is the best thing you can do not only for yourself but for those who love you also. One thing is for sure, always keep God in the midst of all that you do. He talks to us but He speaks gently and you may not hear Him if you do not listen closely so I always ask, Lord show me in a way that I will know that it is You. I am asking Him to speak to me in a way that I understand because He will not speak to me the same way He speaks to you. As I look back over my life, I am so grateful for my brokenness and my mama and granny because they gave me the best they had to give flaws and all. What I choose to do with it is completely up to me. I am excited for all that God has not only in store for me but for you also. I say this to you, be the best you that you can be. God knew us before we were even conceived in the womb and His grace was with us even then. You will not fit in because you were created to stand out. So be Bold but most of all Be You!!

ABOUT THE AUTHOR

Christina L. Worth is very driven, an inspirational speaker, author and mentor that resides in North Dallas with her daughter Amani Victoria. She is vibrant, radical, and impassioned about empowering young ladies. Through her gifts, God birthed Mahogany Angels a Non-Profit organization that Christina serves as the Founder. She strives to encourage, empower, and equip young ladies between the ages of 8-17 years of age from all walks of life to be their best self. Christina has had her share of struggles in the mental realm, but is evolving continually, and is experiencing the victories that come from the renewal of the mind only through God's love. Through her TRUTH, her aspirations are to encourage someone to discover their purpose, passion, and inner strength. When Christina is not changing lives, she enjoys singing, relaxing, and spending quality time with friends and family. For booking information, email **Christina.Worth@yahoo.com.**

www.ingramcontent.com/pod-product-compliance
Lightning Source LLC
Chambersburg PA
CBHW032103040426
42449CB00007B/1174